the ups and downs of

david beckham

scoring brings a full-blooded celebration in a friendly vs. sweden • manchester • november 2001

david

the ups and downs of

beckham

D&C

David and Charles

making headway on england debut in the qualifier vs. moldova • london • september 1996

skipping past a challenge with ease in a friendly vs. saudi arabia • london • may 1998

crossing under pressure during a qualifier vs. moldova • london • october 1997

evading a tackle by roberto di matteo vs. italy in le tournoi de france • nantes • june 1997

shielding the ball in a friendly match vs. saudi arabia • london • may 1998

celebrating alan shearer's world cup goal vs. argentina • st etienne • june 1998

the now infamous clash with diego simeone during the world cup second round match vs. argentina • st etienne • june 1998

… but it's not all plain sailing • chorzow • may 1997

congratulating michael owen on his world cup second round wonder goal vs. argentina • st etienne • june 1998

executing a trademark free kick in the world cup group match vs. colombia • lens • june 1998

defensive duties in a friendly match vs. saudi arabia • london • may 1998

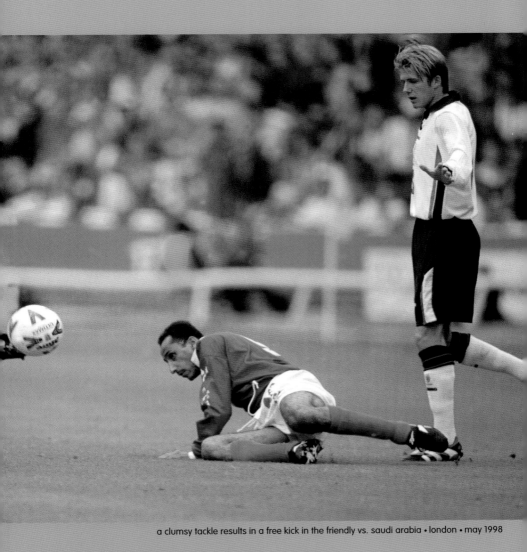

a clumsy tackle results in a free kick in the friendly vs. saudi arabia • london • may 1998

swapping shirts with carlos valderama after england's 2-0 victory in the world cup group match • lens • june 1998

seeing red after a petulant kick on diego simeone during the world cup second round match vs. argentina...

a look of frustration as england draw 0–0 with sweden in a qualifier • london • june 1999

going into the book in a friendly match vs. argentina • london • february 2000

this caution is for a foul on argentina's cristian gonzalez • london • february 2000

a challenge on cristian gonzalez in the friendly vs. argentina • london • february 2000

being helped from the pitch with an injury during a qualifier vs. sweden…

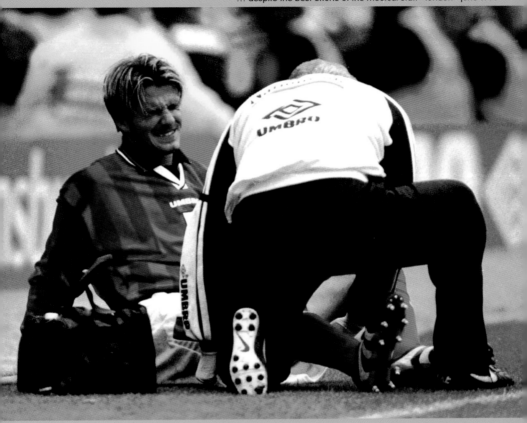

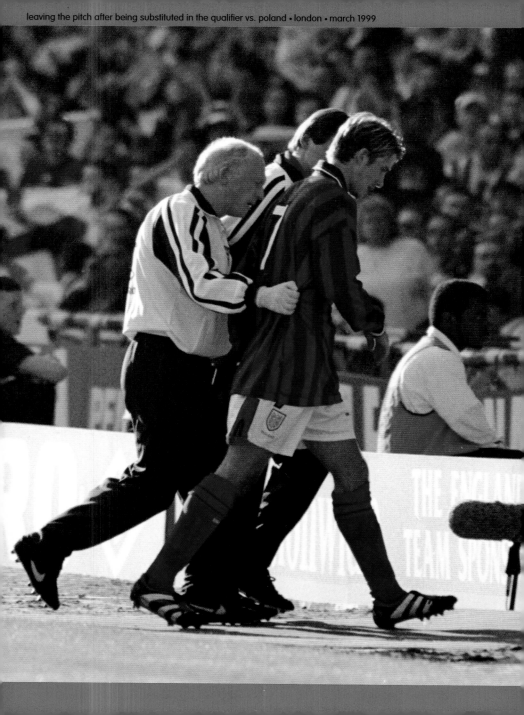

scotland's john collins commits a foul in the euro 2000 play-off match • london • november 1999

being fouled by an argentinian defender in a friendly • london • february 2000

a free kick goes agonisingly close vs. scotland in the euro 2000 play-off game • london • november 1999

disappointment for all at the final whistle after losing 2-0 in a friendly vs. france • london • february 1999

perfect placement in preparation for a corner kick during a friendly vs. brazil • london • may 2000

portugal's luis figo is in close attendance during the euro 2000 group match • eindhoven • june 2000

referee pierluigi collina administers a yellow card during the euro 2000 group match vs. germany • charleroi • june 2000

felled by scotland's john collins during the second leg of the euro 2000 play-off • london • november 1999

up-ended by argentina's rodolfo arruabarrena in a friendly…

... and from another angle • london • february 2000

feeling the pressure after being beaten by portugal in a euro 2000 group match…

... and a controversial reaction to insults from england fans at the end • eindhoven • june 2000

soaking up the patriotic applause after england had defeated scotland 2-0 in the first leg of the euro 2000 play-offs • glasgow • november 1999

ng victory over germany at euro 2000 · charleroi · june 2000

scotland are vanquished · london · november 1999

congratulating david seaman after england claim an aggregate victory over scotland in the euro 2000 play-offs • london • november 1999

a warm handshake for roberto carlos after the friendly clash vs. brazil • london • may 2000

it's all about technique as a free kick is fired in during a qualifier vs. finland • liverpool • march 2001

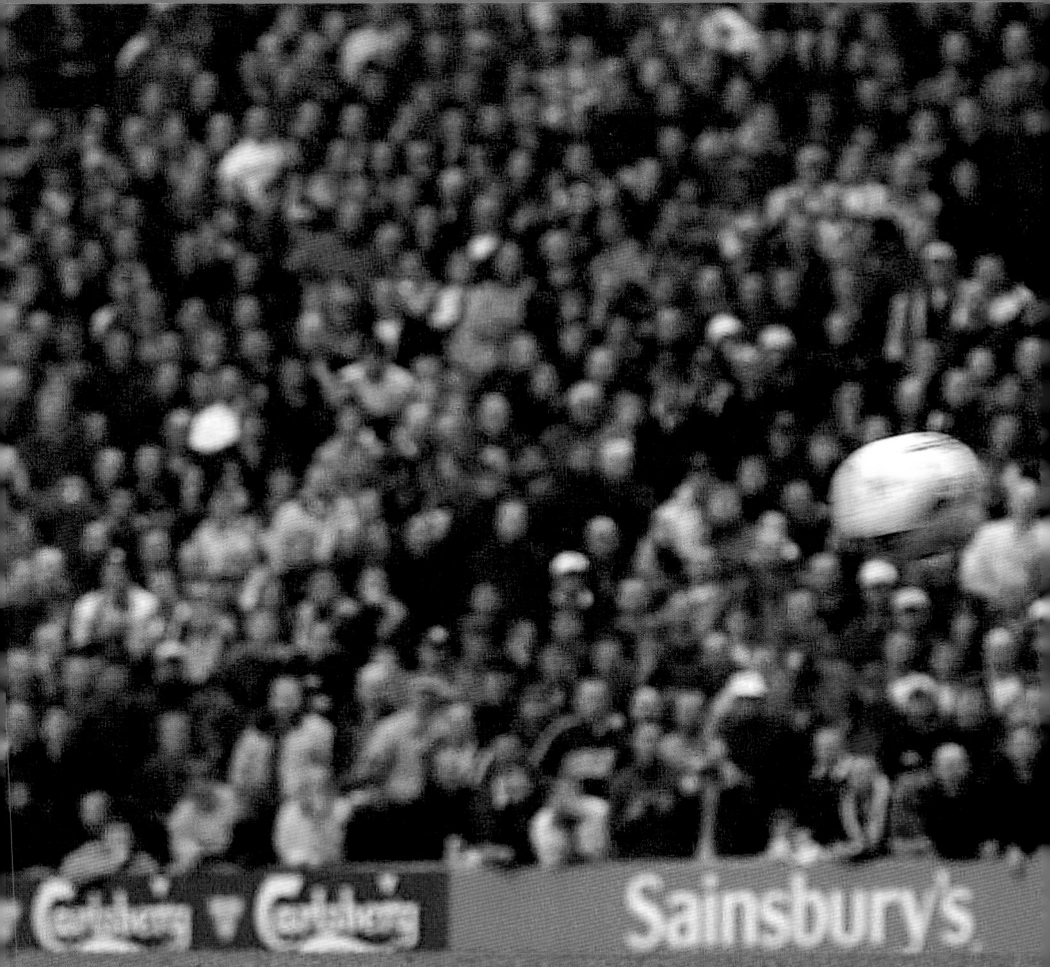
Sainsbury's

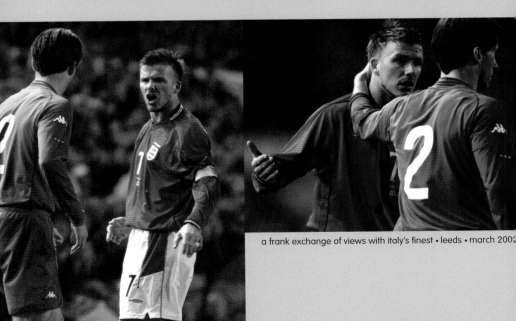

a frank exchange of views with italy's finest • leeds • march 2002

looking for a little divine inspiration during the world cup group match vs. sweden • saitama • june 2002

feeling the pain after being hurt during a friendly vs. holland • amsterdam • february 2002

the pain is clear for all to see in the friendly vs. holland • amsterdam • february 2002

clearly disappointed after being substituted during the world cup group match vs. sweden • saitama • june 2002

taking flight in order to evade a tackle from michael svensson during a friendly vs. sweden • manchester • november 2001

getting airborne during the world cup quarter-final vs. brazil • shizouka • june 2002

sharing a few choice words with italy's gennaro gattuso during a friendly • rome • november 2000

consoling a distraught david seaman after losing the world cup quarter-final to brazil • shizuoka • june 2002

getting defensive with angelos charistea during a qualifier vs. greece • manchester • october 2001

acknowledging the crowd after defeat against brazil in the world cup quarter-final • shizuoka • june 2002

style and guile find the net in a friendly vs. mexico • derby • may 2001

another great try vs. germany in a qualifier • london • october 2000

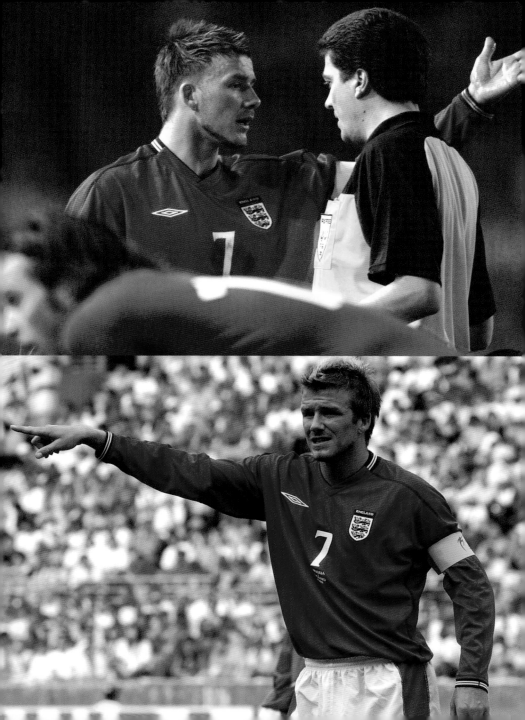

the expression says it all as defeat looms in the world cup quarter-finals vs. brazil • shizuoka • june 2002

gaining the upper hand in a qualifier vs. greece • manchester • october 2001

the last match at wembley ends in disappointment as england lose a qualifier vs. germany • london • october 2000

sheer joy as paul scholes scores against greece in a qualifier • athens • june 2001

observing a minute's silence before a friendly vs. spain • birmingham • february 2001

simply flying after scoring with a superb free kick in the friendly vs. mexico • derby • may 2001

it's time to celebrate in style after scoring the winner in a qualifier vs. finland • liverpool • march 2001

it's all about technique as the winner is slotted home in the world cup group match vs. argentina • japan • june 2002

... as england qualify for the world cup 2002 • manchester • october 2001

closely cropped for the friendly vs. france • paris • september 2000

a mohican style is the order of the day for the friendly vs. mexico • derby • may 2001

one for the fans as england defeat argentina in a world cup group match • sapporo • june 2002

paul scholes is a captivated spectator as that free kick is launched towards greece's goal • manchester • october 2001

wild celebrations after that vital last-gasp equalizer vs. greece in the final qualifier…

... and emile heskey is quick to join the celebrations...

... as england book their place at the world cup • manchester • october 2001

an albanian defender gets the nod during a qualifier • tirana • march 2001

contesting a high ball in a qualifier vs. finland • liverpool • march 2001

getting stuck into a challenge with nigeria's joseph yobo in a world cup group match • osaka • june 2002

attempting to block gennaro gattuso's goal-bound shot in a friendly vs. italy • rome • november 2000

winning the ball cleanly from zlatan ibrahimovic vs. sweden in a friendly • manchester • november 2001

challenged by marcus allbäck in the friendly vs. sweden • manchester • november 2001

out-jumping femi opabunmi in a world cup group match vs. nigeria • osaka • june 2002

not so lucky this time vs. greece in the final qualifier • manchester • october 2001

marking owen's second in the qualifier vs. germany • munich • september 2001

scholes gets the treatment after his goal vs. albania • tirana • march 2001

... even with roberto carlos' shirt • shizuoka • june 2002

being consoled by brazil's ronaldo after the world cup defeat • shizuoka • june 2002

phil neville offers his congratulations after a successful spot kick in the friendly vs. croatia • ipswich • august 2003

... but team-mates intervene before it gets ugly • sunderland • april 2003

preparing to take a penalty in a euro 2004 group match vs. france • lisbon • june 2004 down but not out after being felled in a friendly vs. denmark • manchester • november 2003

curling a trademark free kick in off the post in a qualifier vs. liechtenstein • vaduz • march 2003

spot kick success in a friendly vs. croatia • ipswich • august 2003

fabio d'elia challenges in a qualifier vs. liechtenstein • vaduz • march 2003

holding off a marker during a euro 2004 group match vs. croatia • lisbon • june 2004

in the thick of the action in a friendly vs. japan • manchester • june 2004

the one that got away in the final qualifier vs. turkey • istanbul • october 2003

guiding a free kick into the net in a qualifier vs. liechtenstein • vaduz • march 2003

down on hands and knees in the euro 2004 group match vs. france • lisbon • june 2004

previous page • it's all too much after being beaten by portugal in the euro 2004 quarter-finals • lisbon • june 2004

... and the ball is on target • vaduz • march 2003

a clean strike in the qualifier vs. liechtenstein...

trying to bend a free kick into the net during the friendly vs. croatia • ipswich • august 2003

sparks fly with turkey's alpay in the final qualifier • istanbul • october 2003

respect for france's zinedine zidane in a euro 2004 group match • lisbon • june 2004

lying injured after receiving a knock in the friendly vs. japan • manchester • june 2004

eye on the ball in the qualifier vs. liechtenstein • vaduz • march 2003

surface concerns before taking a penalty in the euro 2004 quarter-final vs. portugal • lisbon • june 2004

lots to think about as england are beaten 3-2 in a friendly vs. denmark • manchester • november 2003

right on target in a friendly vs. croatia • ipswich • august 2003

one for the collection as turkey are beaten 2-0 in a qualifier • sunderland • april 2003

looking for some justice in the qualifier vs. liechtenstein • vaduz • march 2003

taking the applause after scoring in the qualifier vs. liechenstein • vaduz • march 2003

long faces with ledley king after being beaten by france in the euro 2004 group match • lisbon • june 2004

all smiles with rio ferdinand after scoring in the friendly vs. croatia • ipswich • august 2003

plenty to shout about with steven gerrard in the euro 2004 group match vs. switzerland…

the referee awards a free kick in the qualifier vs. liechtenstein • vaduz • march 2003

running repairs in the qualifier vs liechtenstein • vaduz • march 2003

some fine adjustments during the final qualifier vs. turkey • istanbul • october 2003

alpay is quick to comment after the penalty miss vs. turkey in the final qualifier • istanbul • october 2003

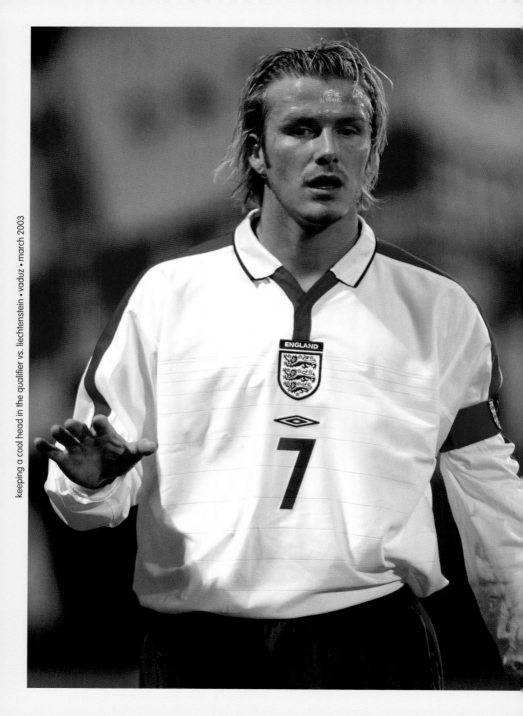

keeping a cool head in the qualifier vs. liechtenstein · vaduz · march 2003

challenging mario frick in the qualifier vs. liechtenstein • manchester • september 2003

time to celebrate after scoring vs. liechtenstein • vaduz • march 2003

getting the jump on portugal's rui jorge in a friendly • faro loulé • february 2004

first to the ball in a challenge with bixente lizarazu of france in the euro 2004 group match · lisbon · june 2004

penalty success vs. croatia • ipswich • august 2003

the big thumbs up as england defeat switzerland 3–0 in a euro 2004 group match • coimbra • june 2004

disallowed vs. turkey in a qualifier • istanbul • october 2003

home and dry vs. turkey • sunderland • april 2003

so close vs. macedonia in a qualifier...

… and the disappointment is clear to see • southampton • october 2002

tired and dejected after losing to portugal in the euro 2004 quarter-finals • lisbon • june 2004

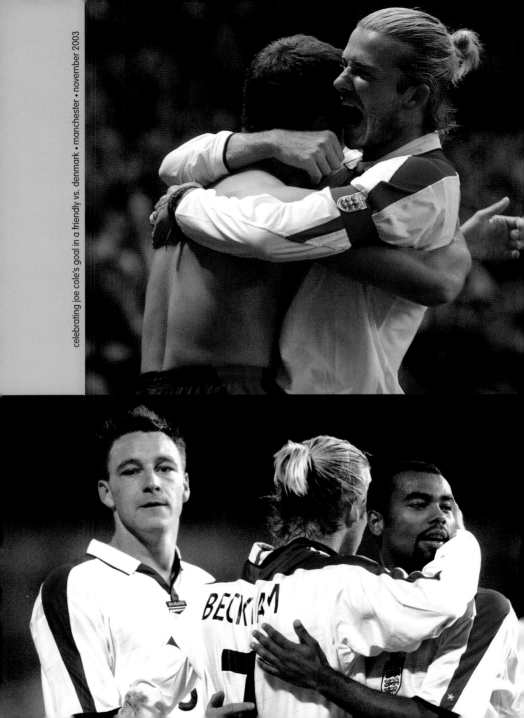

embracing wayne rooney as england beat turkey in a qualifier • sunderland • april 2003

running with the ball in a qualifier vs. liechtenstein • vaduz • march 2003

pride and passion after scoring the equalizer vs. macedonia in a qualifier • southampton • october 2002

a moment's contemplation during a friendly vs. denmark • manchester • november 2003

feeling the full force of thabang molefe's challenge in a friendly vs. south africa...

… but molefe got a touch on the ball • durban • may 2003

smiles all round as michael owen equalizes in a qualifier vs. slovakia...

... and the captain is delighted • bratislava • october 2002

not a good day as england lose to australia in a friendly · london · february 2003

receiving treatment during the friendly vs. japan · manchester · june 2004

talking tactics with sven goran eriksson before the qualifier vs. macedonia • skopje • september 2003

gary neville offers consolation after defeat at the hands of france in the euro 2004 group match • lisbon • june 2004

missing a crucial shoot-out penalty in the euro 2004 quarter-finals vs. portugal • lisbon • june 2004

leaving the fray early with a handshake for ben thatcher in the qualifier vs. wales • manchester • october 2004

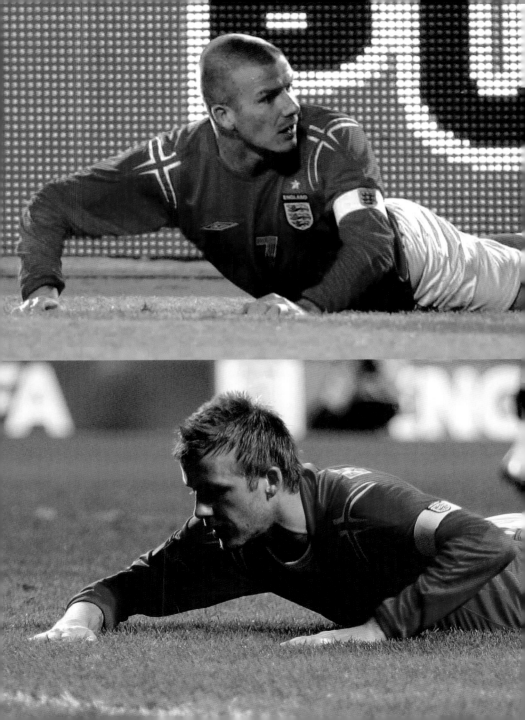

flat out in the qualifier vs. poland • chorzow • september 2004

back to earth in a friendly vs. holland • birmingham • february 2005

delight at opening the scoring in a friendly vs. ukraine…

... but help is soon at hand • manchester • september 2004

going head-to-head during a friendly vs. holland • birmingham • february 2005

another dead ball situation during a qualifier vs. azerbaijan...

...as the ball is guided home...

...the outcome is yet another success • newcastle • march 2005

fearing the worst with injury during the qualifier vs. wales • manchester • october 2004

lapping it up after scoring against wales in a qualifier • manchester • october 2004

taking the knocks during a friendly vs. spain • madrid • november 2004

competing with rafael van der vaart in a friendly vs. holland…

... and taking evasive action by vaulting over a challenge from van der vaart • birmingham • february 2005

a quick handshake for david james after the 2-2 qualifying draw vs. austria • vienna • september 2004

battling for possession with former club-mate ryan giggs during the qualifier vs. wales • manchester • october 2004

injury forces an early withdrawal in the qualifier vs. wales • manchester • october 2004

greeted by the boss after being substituted during the qualifier vs. northern ireland • manchester • march 2005 a captain's duel with gary speed of wales during the qualifier…

starting the celebrations after scoring vs. wales in the qualifier • manchester • october 2004

this nudge on austria's dietmar kuhbauer brings a yellow card during a qualifier • vienna • september 2004

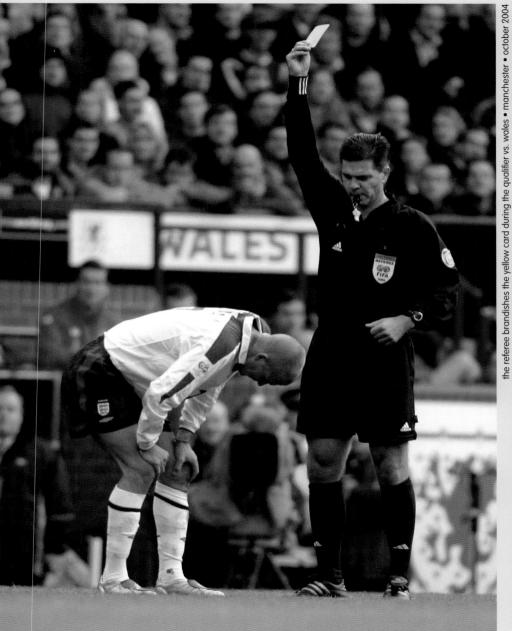

the joy is obvious after scoring in the qualifier vs. wales • manchester • october 2004

rooney needs restraining vs. northern ireland • belfast • september 2005

the referee blows his whistle and confirms a disasterous 1-0 defeat to northern ireland • belfast • september 2005

the northern ireland manager offers commiserations after an unlikely victory for his team • belfast • september 2005

winning a header against andreas ibertsberger in the qualifier vs. austria...

... but the raised arm earns a harsh booking • manchester • october 2005

a tangling of feet with andreas ibertsberger
in the qualifier vs. austria…

... and it's a second red in an england shirt
• manchester • october 2005

joining the huddle as owen equalizes vs. argentina • geneva • november 2005

rooney gives the captain a lift after his goal vs. argentina • geneva • november 2005 tight marking from the argentine left back • geneva • november 2005

sweet victory against old rivals argentina • geneva • november 2005

photo credits:
all images © mirrorpix
except: pages 6, 9, 14, 15,
19, 36, 39, 50, 61, 137(b), 180(b),
190(b), 194, 195, 202, 209(t)
© action images

a david & charles book
copyright © david & charles 2006

first published in the uk in 2006

david & charles is an
f+w publications inc. company
4700 east galbraith road
cincinnati, oh 45236

a catalogue record for this book is
available from the british library

isbn-13: 978-0-7153-2439-4
isbn-10: 0-7153-2439-X

printed in china by snp leefung
for david & charles
brunel house newton abbot devon

commissioning editor neil baber
editor jennifer proverbs
art editor mike moule
production controller kelly smith

www.davidandcharles.co.uk

david & charles books are available from
all good bookshops; alternatively you can
contact our orderline on 0870 9908222
or write to us at freepost EX2 110, d&c
direct, newton abbot, tq12 4zz (no stamp
required uk only); us customers call
800-289-0963 and canadian customers
call 800-840-5220.